GW00938042

DINOSAUR HEROES & VILLAINS

Dinosaurs ruled the earth for about 165 million years. They have fascinated people for hundreds of years, which is why there are so many myths and legends surrounding these fantastic creatures. There are many famous stories and films about dinosaurs and some of these exciting tales are based on fact, but others are pure fantasy. Let's find out what the dinosaurs were really like.

This book explains about the dinosaurs in a way that is clear and easy to understand, separating fact from fiction. At the same time you will enjoy the fun games, colouring in and activities.

Contents

Written by William Webb
Illustrated by Mark Hoolahan and Les Ives
Published by Colour History Ltd © 2008
Print reference number 31090/11/08

What is a Dinosaur?

Dinosaurs were reptiles with straight legs and they lived 230 to 65 million years ago. They were not swimming reptiles, flying reptiles or reptiles which walked with bent legs like crocodiles.

The British scientist Richard Owen invented the name 'Dinosauria' in 1842 and this is where we get the word dinosaur from. There are many features which make a reptile a dinosaur and here are some of them:

- **Dinosaurs stand on their toes and this is called a 'digitigrade posture'**

- **They have a special hip joint, knee joint and ankle joint**

- **They have more than three joined 'sacral' or hip vertebrae between the hip bones**

When Did Dinosaurs Live?
Dinosaurs appeared around the late Triassic period, which was about 230 million years ago. They existed until the end of the Cretaceous period about 65 million years ago, during the Mesozoic era. Dinosaurs lived all over the world. Small mammals lived at the same time as dinosaurs, but they did not dominate the earth until the dinosaurs died out.

Dinosaur Remains
One of the main ways we can find out about dinosaurs is through their fossilised bones. There are all sorts of fossils, including trees and forests, plants, insects, seashells, mammals, dinosaur bones, eggs, footprints, skin impressions, stomach stones, bacteria, fungi and even dinosaur poo!

Make A Fossil
Collect some large leaves and place a piece of paper over one of them. Gently rub a pencil, or crayon over the paper and you will leave an impression of the leaf on the paper. It will look like the thin carbon fossil impressions of prehistoric leaves.

Dino Detective
The picture below shows a Stegosaurus, a plesiosaur, an Edaphosaurus and a pterosaur. Write their names in the spaces provided. Read the bold introduction paragraph above again and tick the ones you think are dinosaurs.

1 _____   2 _____

3 _____   4 _____

Answers: 1. pterosaur 2. plesiosaur 3. Edaphosaurus 4. Stegosaurus. Stegosaurus is the only one that is a dinosaur.

How Do Fossils Form?

The hardest parts of an animal become fossilised, such as the teeth, skeleton or shell. On rare occasions a soft, fleshy part might be fossilised. Some fossils can be formed when volcanic ash covers an animal, or when resin oozes from a tree and turns into amber, trapping a small animal like an insect or a frog.

Fossils can also form when tar seeps from the ground and hardens over a trapped animal. This only preserves them for thousands of years, not millions. The most common way for fossils to form is when something is covered with sand, mud or clay, which turns to rock over time.

The diagram opposite shows how fossils are formed.

1. An animal dies, falls to the ground and is eaten by scavengers and broken down by bacteria.

2. The hard skeleton is left which may break down over time.

3. However, a storm for example, could sweep in a layer of mud over the skeleton.

4. Over millions of years other layers of sediment are deposited, which harden under pressure. The skeleton breaks down due to acid in underground water, leaving an empty skeleton-shaped 'mould'.

5. Water seeps into the mould and leaves minerals, which harden into a 'cast' of the mould. In the case of bones, they can be replaced with other minerals.

6. Wind and water erode the sedimentary rock which exposes the fossil. Landslides or quarrying can also reveal fossils.

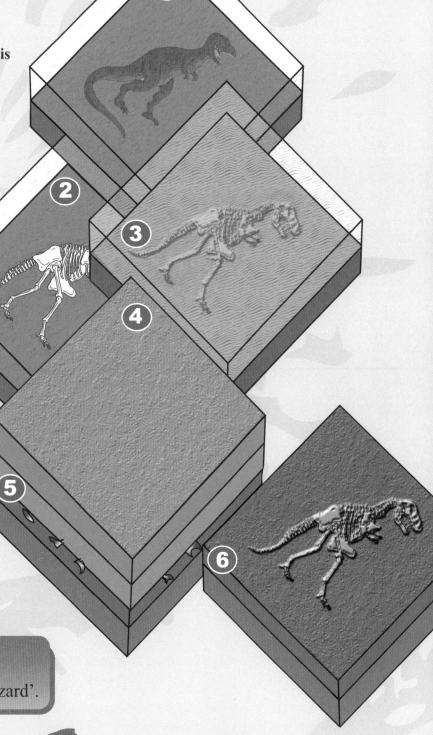

Did you know?
The word dinosaur means 'terrible lizard'.

How Do We Know About Dinosaurs?

The fossil bones of dinosaurs can tell scientists a great deal, but there are many other ways of finding out about dinosaurs and the world they lived in, what they looked like and how they lived.

The Matrix

The sedimentary rock surrounding a fossil is called the 'matrix'. The matrix can give scientists important clues about where a dinosaur lived. If there are seashells then they lived by the sea, or if all the bones are jumbled up they may have arrived there after a storm. It can also tell scientists how old the dinosaur fossil is. Once all the clues have been studied, the bones can be removed from the matrix.

Rare Animal Remains

Sometimes the skin, flesh, fur, hair and feathers of prehistoric animals have been found. This can happen if the soft parts were preserved before bacteria destroyed them.

Trace Fossils

Trace fossils are evidence of animal life, but not the animals themselves. Footprints of dinosaurs have survived from when they walked in mud. Where there are lots of footprints, called a 'trackway', scientists can tell how quickly a dinosaur moved by the distance between the footprints.

What did dinosaurs eat?

Dinosaurs had different kinds of teeth just like modern animals do. Those that ate fish had straight, cone-shaped teeth. Meat-eaters had large, curved, sharp teeth, sometimes with jagged edges. Plant-eaters had lots of teeth with large grinding surfaces, or spoon-shaped teeth for stripping leaves off branches.

Sometimes scientists are lucky enough to find the fossilised content of the stomach, fossilised poo called 'coprolites', or a tooth from an attacking dinosaur. Coprolites and stomach contents can be studied for evidence of crushed bones, or the minerals which are found in plants. Some plant-eaters may have used stones to grind tough plants down and these are called 'gastroliths'. These smooth stones may give us clues about how dinosaurs behaved and where they lived.

Dinosaur Eggs

The discovery of several nests of dinosaur eggs has led scientists to believe that dinosaurs incubated their young. Later dinosaurs nested in colonies on the ground. The largest eggs are about 30 cm long, from which a 30 metre long dinosaur weighing about 20 tonnes would grow. Some of the eggs contain fossil embryos. You can see a nest of fossilised dinosaur eggs, which were found in outer Mongolia, China, at the Dinosaur Museum at **Combe Martin Wildlife and Dinosaur Park**.

Fossilised dinosaur eggs

Shapes and Sizes

Bones are normally smooth, but where muscles and tendons were attached there are often rough patches. By studying these it is possible to work out the shape and size of a muscle and therefore how powerful the dinosaur was.

Did you know?

Oil is the remains of animals and plants formed in the sea? Coal is actually dead fossil plants and animals compressed over time which has turned into carbon, this is why it burns so well. Gas is formed from rotting vegetation.

T-rex Lives!

In the film 'Jurassic Park', DNA was taken from prehistoric mosquitoes trapped in amber shortly after they had sucked out some dinosaur blood. This was used to clone living dinosaurs like T-rex. Could scientists today implant this DNA into a living egg? No! There is not enough surviving DNA to create a dinosaur.

Did you know?

Combe Martin Wildlife and Dinosaur Park in North Devon has a full size T-rex, which is operated using the latest animatronic technology. It's scary so you should prepare yourself for an experience you will not forget. They also have two vicious interacting Megalosaurs, a Velociraptor and a Dilophosaurus, 'the Spitting Dinosaur'.

Bring Back Dinosaurs!

DNA is a chemical found in living cells and it determines what cells grow into. For instance, whether they become a man or an elephant. If it was possible to extract the DNA of a dinosaur from a fossil, do you think scientists should be allowed to recreate a dinosaur?

What Were Dinosaurs Like?

Scientists don't know exactly what dinosaurs looked like, but they can compare them to similar animals today. Fossil evidence helps them to piece together what they could have looked like.

Appearance

Dinosaur skin impressions have been found which show rough skin textures. The skin of a duck-billed dinosaur was recently unearthed in America. It has different-sized scales, which in modern reptiles can represent different colours.

Bone Structure

Dinosaurs looked very different to humans, but they had similar bones. For example, they had one large bone in the upper arm and two small bones in the lower arm. Scientists think birds may have evolved from theropods, or flesh-eating dinosaurs because their skeletons are very similar.

Walk like a Dinosaur

Dinosaurs either walked on their back feet or on all fours. The elephant-like Diplodocus was probably able to stand up on its back legs using its tail as a prop, so that it could reach higher plants. Some may have travelled in herds like cattle, with the young in the centre of the herd for protection. A meat-eater like Allosaurus might have preyed on weak or young animals, or could have hunted in packs.

Dinosaur Sprint

T-rex could have been capable of running up to 29 km per hour over short distances to catch prey, but it may have been able to trot for longer distances.

Were Dinosaurs Cold or Warm-Blooded?

It was once thought that dinosaurs were cold-blooded 'ectotherms' because they evolved from reptiles. Now some scientists believe they could have been warm-blooded 'endotherms' like birds.

Evidence for cold-blooded

- Dinosaurs look like cold-blooded lizards and reptiles
- Heat loss would be reduced in large animals like dinosaurs

Evidence for warm-blooded

- The largest animals of today are warm-blooded
- Dinosaur bones have a warm-blooded structure
- Dinosaurs stood erect, not sprawled like lizards and this is only seen in warm-blooded animals
- Some dinosaurs had insulation like warm-blooded animals do
- Dinosaurs grew up fast, which is only possible for warm-blooded animals
- Dinosaur young look different to their adults, like warm-blooded animals. Cold-blooded young look like smaller versions of their adults
- Dinosaurs had large chests like warm-blooded animals
- Some lived in arctic conditions, which is only possible for warm-blooded animals
- Some dinosaurs were nocturnal, but cold-blooded animals need sunlight to be active
- Some dinosaurs digested their food quickly, like warm-blooded animals

Create a Dinosaur

Look at some pictures of modern reptiles, such as lizards and snakes and using the space below create your own dinosaur.

The Dinosaur World

When dinosaurs first appeared on the earth there were fewer types of animals, although mammals were evolving at about the same time. There were no flowers or grass, but instead lots of ferns and mosses. So, the world looked less colourful than it does today.

Dull Triassic Times
Scientists have found evidence of the same animals and plants all over the world at the beginning of the dinosaur period. So, they believe that all of the land masses were originally joined together. By studying sedimentary rocks, they think that the centre of this giant land mass was mainly desert, with some greener areas containing lots of plants.

Colourful Jurassic and Cretaceous Times
By the late Jurassic period wildlife appeared in greater varieties. The first flowers blossomed in the early Cretaceous. The climate was very humid with wet and dry seasons. The largest pterosaurs to fly in the skies lived during the Cretaceous and with wingspans of up to 14 metres, they were the size of a small aeroplane!

At the end of the Cretaceous the world would have looked more like it does today, with a greater variety of plant life, some simple grasses and colourful feathered dinosaurs and birds.

The Garden of England
The earliest known fossil flower was found in southern England.

Life in the Sea
Fish reptiles called 'ichthyosaurs', which looked a bit like dolphins, appeared before the first dinosaurs in the early Triassic. Later, long-necked plesiosaurs with flippers and tails arrived. Some people believe that the Loch Ness Monster, if it ever existed, was a plesiosaur.

What Happened to the Dinosaurs?

At the end of the Cretaceous period the dinosaurs disappeared. Scientists believe it was the fifth mass extinction since life began on earth. However, no one knows for certain why dinosaurs died out, but there are several possible reasons:

Climate Change
In the late Cretaceous the climate was getting warmer and a rise in sea level reduced their habitat.

Asteroid Collision
A 10 km wide asteroid hit Mexico triggering forest fires, tsunamis and a cold winter. This would have killed off dinosaurs and other animals. This theory is based on the discovery of a crater and minerals commonly found in meteorites.

Volcanic Eruptions
Dramatic environmental changes may have occurred due to massive volcanic activity in what is now India.

Problems with the theories

Scientists have not been able to agree with one theory, because there are several problems with them:

- Why did the successful dinosaurs die out, whilst frogs, which are not as good at survival, live on?
- Perhaps dinosaurs did not die out suddenly, but simply faded away as other species have done, due to gradual environmental changes.
- Scientists cannot accurately date events which happened so long ago.

Scientists today think a combination of the asteroid and volcanic eruptions could have caused the extinction of the dinosaurs. What do you think happened?

Spot the Odd Ones Out

Look at this picture and circle anything that you think would not have existed when dinosaurs roamed the earth.

Colour in this dinosaur scene

11

Dinosaur Shapes and Sizes

All animals adapt to the environment they live in. This is why dinosaurs were different shapes and sizes. On this page you can read about some of the weird and wonderful dinosaurs which have been discovered.

Duck-Billed dinosaurs

Duck-billed dinosaurs lived near water and used their beaks to feed on tough plants. Some, like Parasaurolophus, had crests on their heads, which contained winding nasal passages. Their crests may have been brightly coloured in order to attract females using a mating dance.

Fringed-Heads

'Fringed-heads' were plant-eaters with a shelf or frill at the back of their skull. They included Protoceratops and the three-horned Triceratops. They were similar to modern rhinoceroses, but they had beaks and were much bigger.

Dino-Tanks

These included heavily armoured plant-eating dinosaurs like Stegosaurus and Ankylosaurus. Ankylosaurus used its medieval mace-like tail to club an opponent to death.

Dino-Birds

Feathered 'dino-birds' like the Archaeopteryx below could fly short distances. Their feathers kept them warm. If they were brightly coloured they may have been used for display.

Sauropods

Huge plant-eating sauropods ate vast quantities of food. Scientists have studied the teeth of the largest plant-eaters and they think that they were able to eat food at different heights. This meant that there was less competition for food.

Theropods

Theropods were mainly flesh-eating dinosaurs like Tyrannosaurus. They were often characterised by their powerful hind legs for running and their huge teeth, which they used to rip open their prey.

Ostrich Dinosaurs

Ostrich dinosaurs looked similar to modern ostriches and could run up to 60 km per hour. Scientists can usually tell what food a dinosaur ate by its teeth, but these theropods did not have teeth. They were probably plant-eaters because they were very common. Meat-eaters are fewer in number and stomach stones (see page 5) have been found in their tummies.

Remember!

Dinosaurs lived at different times, so when you see films like 'King Kong' and 'Jurassic Park', you need to remember that some of those scenes would never have happened. A Stegosaurus never saw a Tyrannosaurus, because Tyrannosaurus didn't appear until 80 or so million years following the extinction of the Stegosaurus. The same is true for Apatosaurus, which used to be called a 'Brontosaurus'. They died out long before the Tyrannosaurus roamed the earth.

Dinosaur Giants

The biggest dinosaurs to roam the earth date from the early Cretaceous. The plant-eating Argentinosaurus may have been 21 metres tall, 35 metres long and weighed between 75 and 100 tonnes. When it walked around, the ground must have shook!

The largest predator dinosaur was called Giganotosaurus. It was 14 metres in length and weighed around 6 to 8 tonnes. Its skull alone was over 1.6 metres long.

Amazing Dinosaurs

Help the baby dinosaurs find their friends who are lost in the middle of the maze.

Name the Dinosaur

Look at the dinosaurs below and write the number of each dinosaur in the circle next to the correct dinosaur name.

Eoraptor   Apatosaurus   Archaeopteryx   Triceratops   T-rex

Answers: 1. T-rex 2. Archaeopteryx 3. Triceratops 4. Apatosaurus 5. Eoraptor

Meat-eaters

One of the most famous and terrifying meat-eaters was Tyrannosaurus rex, whose name means 'tyrant king of the lizards'.

This 12 metre long beast lived during the late Cretaceous period. Its mouth could open a metre wide, revealing an array of huge teeth the size and shape of bananas. It probably hunted prey, as it was powerfully built and had an awesome bite. However, some scientists think it could have been slower and it may have lived on the scraps left over by other animals.

Velociraptor

Tyrannosaurus rex

Velociraptor caught in the act!

Velociraptor means 'fast robber' and they lived at the same time as Tyrannosaurus. An amazing fossil of this flesh-eater caught it in the act of killing a fringed-headed Protoceratops. The Velociraptor had killed the Protoceratops with its deadly sickle-shaped claws, but one of its arms was trapped in its prey's beaked jaws, so it could not escape. Velociraptor claws were so sharp that they could rip open a victim's body easily.

Megalosaurus

Megalosaurus, meaning 'big lizard', was one of the first dinosaurs to be discovered. In 1676 a leg bone was found and described as the bone of a giant. Originally it was thought to be four-legged. There is a life-size Victorian sculpture of one in this pose in Crystal Palace Park, London. We now know that the 9 metre long Megalosaurus was two-legged and lived during the Middle Jurassic. It probably preyed on Stegosaurus.

Film Becomes Fact

Velociraptor was the height of a man and about the weight of a wolf. In the movie 'Jurassic Park', Velociraptor was shown as a much larger creature. However, during the making of the film, a big raptor was found in North America. Since then more large raptors have been discovered in Argentina, Japan and elsewhere in Asia.

Megalosaurus

What do you think?

Large predators like lions and hyenas scavenge meat when it is available, but they prefer fresh meat. Now consider the evidence below and decide whether you think T-rex was a scavenger or a predator.

Was T-rex a SCAVENGER?

■ T-rex had small eyes making it difficult to see prey
■ Tyrannosaurus had a good sense of smell to detect dead animals, just like vultures
■ Its legs were built for walking long distances in search of dead animals.

...or was it a PREDATOR?

■ It had binocular eyesight, ideal for hunting
■ Bones have been found with T-rex teeth stuck in them
■ T-rex had huge jaws and bone-crushing teeth to kill its prey
■ Its legs were powerful, so it could have run fast to catch prey

Create a 3D Dinosaur World

Cut a slit about 1 x 4 cm in the centre of the short end of a shoe box. This is your peephole. At the opposite end stick a drawing of a dinosaur world on the inside of the box. Cut one or two windows about 4 cm square on both long sides of the box and three long slits at equal intervals in the lid. These windows will let light in. Between the windows inside the box, stick card dinosaurs and plants projecting from the sides to form a 3D landscape. Put the lid on the box, look through the peephole and wonder at the dinosaur world you have created!

Spot the Difference

Spot 8 differences between the two pictures below.

Plant-eaters

Some plant-eaters were the largest animals that ever roamed the earth, particularly the sauropods. There was a wide variety of plant-eaters, including fringed-heads, armoured dinosaurs, duck-billed dinosaurs and possibly some theropods.

Apatosaurus

The Apatosaurus, meaning 'deceptive lizard', lived during the late Jurassic. It grew to about 24 metres in length, was about 9 metres high and weighed nearly 23 tonnes. It had a brain the size of a computer mouse. Its tail had 82 bones and was as heavy as three grand pianos! It was previously thought that the tail dragged on the ground, but it probably acted like a counter-balance to its extremely long neck. It's tail could have been used like a whip when it was defending itself from a predator, like Allosaurus.

Stegosaurus

Stegosaurus, which means 'roof lizard', lived at the same time as Apatosaurus. This 9 metre long, 4 metre tall, plate-backed dinosaur had spikes in its tail, which might have been used for defence. The grooves in its plates may have been blood vessels. So any wound to the plates would have caused massive bleeding, making it unlikely that they were used for defence. Instead, Stegosaurus may have used its plates in mating displays, or to scare off meat-eaters. Other kinds of stegosaurs had rows of spikes on their backs instead of plates.

Did you know?

This new thinking meant that the 100 year old Diplodocus replica skeleton in the **Natural History Museum, London** had to be dismantled and repositioned!

Stegosaurus

Apatosaurus

Triceratops

Triceratops means 'three-horned face'. This late Cretaceous fringed-head was about 9 metres long. It looked like a cross between an elephant and a rhinocerous. It may have used its horns and frills in competition for females, as well as in defence against a Tyrannosaurus. Perhaps it locked horns like African antelope do, pushing its opponent until it surrendered. The horns and frills may have helped Triceratops to recognise its own kind. Triceratops probably lived in large herds, like modern elephants or zebras.

Triceratops

Dinosaur Graveyards

Most dinosaur bones are found one at a time. It is rare for scientists to find a nearly complete skeleton. Finding the fossils of dozens of dinosaurs is like winning the lottery. Fossil remains of horned dinosaurs have often been found in 'dinosaur graveyards'.

Why dinosaur graveyards? Usually the victims died at the same time. They might have been killed crossing a river, or after a volcanic eruption. Dinosaurs found grouped together like this may have lived in herds.

Euoplocephalus

Euoplocephalus means 'well-armoured head'. It would have roamed the earth with Triceratops and Tyrannosaurus, but it was smaller than Triceratops. It was covered in bony plates, horns and spikes, which formed a suit of armour from head to tail.

Euoplocephalus

Hunting Dinosaurs

We have known about fossils since ancient times. They were thought to be the remains of mythical creatures or giants. People believed that they could offer protection from evil spirits and had healing properties. Fossils are still used in Chinese medicine today.

Evolution

An English canal engineer called William Smith saw that rock layers around England contained the same kinds of fossils, in the same layer, no matter where he found them. In 1859 Charles Darwin published his 'Origin of Species'. This stated that fossils were extinct animals and that living things alter and adapt to the changing environment, or they die.

The Golden Age of Dinosaur Hunting

Sir Richard Owen was the first person to use the word 'Dinosauria' to describe what he called 'fearfully great reptiles'. The late 1800's were the 'golden age' of dinosaur discovery and many of the dinosaurs we know today were first found then. Today, there is a fresh revival of dinosaur finds, especially in countries like China.

Palaeontology - The Study Of Fossils

The word 'fossil' used to mean 'something dug up', but today it means the remains, or evidence of prehistoric life. 'Palaeontology' is the study of fossils, ancient extinct life and their past environments. Someone who collects and studies fossils is called a palaeontologist. Palaeontologists use fossils to reconstruct the history of the earth and life on the planet. Some palaeontologists work for the oil industry, because they know about sedimentary rocks. Others study past climates and environments to understand global warming, cooling and climate change.

Mary Anning (1799-1847)

Mary Anning was born on the south coast of England at Lyme Regis in Dorset, which has cliffs rich in Jurassic fossils. Her father was a cabinet-maker who collected and sold fossils as a hobby. Around the time her father died, when she was about twelve years old, Mary and her brother found the first complete ichthyosaur skeleton.

Mary made many great discoveries, including the first plesiosaur and a pterosaur. Her fossils were sought by museums and scientists. She was granted an annual payment for her work and she was made an honorary member of the Geological Society of London. Lady Harriet Sivester wrote in her diary after visiting Mary, 'they (scientists) all acknowledge that she understands more of the science than anyone else in this kingdom'.

Did you know?

Mary Anning could not become a full member of the Geological Society of London because she was a woman.

Fossil Hunting

Some fossils can be picked up on a beach in the shingle, such as at Bognor Regis. Southwold is a good place to find amber. Check under rocks or under a cliff at Hastings, where fossils will have fallen following a high tide or storm. Always take a parent or guardian and never attempt to climb cliffs, as this can be very dangerous.

Did you know?

The 'Jurassic Coast' is the only site in the world that spans the whole of the Mesozoic era. This is why it has been made a World Heritage Site. It stretches from Orcombe Point near Exmouth in East Devon to Old Harry Rocks near Swanage in East Dorset, a distance of 153 kms.

Geological Timeline & Glossary

Eon	Era	Millions of Years	Time Period	Major Events
Phanerozoic	Cenozoic		**Quaternary:** Holocene Pliestocene **Neogene:** Pliocene Miocene **Palaeogene:** Oligocene Eocene Paleocene	*Rise of human civilisation* *Ice age* *Early man* *All life forms appear in greater variety*
		65		
	MESOZOIC era of dinosaurs		Cretaceous	*Dinosaurs and ammonites extinct*
			Jurassic	*Flowers, sharks Tyrannosaurus, fringed-headed, duck-billed and largest sauropods* *Stegosaurs and sauropods, birds* *Many reptiles, first mammals, large sea creatures and flying reptiles*
		248	Triassic	
	Palaeozoic		Permian	*Extinctions of many sea & land animals*
			Carboniferous	
			Devonian	*Early amphibians*
			Silurian	*Plants and trees, insects and marine life*
			Ordivician	
		543	Cambrian	
Precambrian	Proterozoic		Neoproterozoic	*First animals*
			Mesoproterozoic	*Continents form*
		2500	Paleoproterozoic	
	Archaean			*Earliest forms of life*
		3800		*Land forms as the earth cools*
	Hadean			*The earth forms*
		4500		*Birth of the solar system*

Glossary

Amber Orange fossil resin or tree sap often used in jewellery

Ammonite Fossilised squid-like sea creature that lived in a shell

Bacteria Microscopic cells which live everywhere

Carbon A chemical element present in all life forms and occurs naturally as diamonds, coal, graphite or fossils

Coprolite Fossilised dinosaur poo

Cretaceous Geological time period after the Jurassic period

Digitigrade Animals like birds, dogs and cats that walk on their toes

Dinosauria Group of prehistoric reptiles that have upright legs and do not include flying or swimming reptiles

DNA Deoxyribonucleic acid which is found in every life form and provides instructions for how they will grow

Early Triassic, Jurassic or Cretaceous Means 'at the start of' and is also called 'Lower Triassic, Jurassic or Cretaceous'

Ectotherms Animals relying on outside heat to keep warm

Embryo The earliest stage in animal growth before the egg hatches

Endotherms Animals which can maintain their own body heat

Eon Long period of time divided into eras

Era Time between major extinctions of wildlife

Fossil Remains of an animal or plant found in sedimentary rock layers

Fungi Mainly invisible plant-like growth which includes yeast, mould and mushrooms

Gastrolith Smooth stones used by plant-eating dinosaurs to help them grind down strong plants

Homology Study of similarities in the anatomy of creatures as they evolved over time

Incubate Keeping an egg warm as the embryo inside develops, usually with body heat, but it can be by covering the egg

Jurassic Geological time period after the Triassic

Late Triassic, Jurassic or Cretaceous Means 'towards the end of', also called 'Upper Triassic, Jurassic or Cretaceous'

Mesozoic Geological era when the dinosaurs lived

Mineral A solid which has formed because of geological events

Nocturnal An animal which is active during the night

Palaeontology Study of prehistoric life using fossil evidence

Prehistoric The time from the beginning of the world up to when history was first written down

Pterosaur A flying reptile

Sacral Bones located between the hip bones

Sauropod Large four-legged, plant-eating dinosaurs

Sediment Material left by water or wind

Sedimentary rock Rocks formed when pressure from deposited sediment crushes sediment underneath, forming layers which contain fossils

Species Living things put into groups according to how similar they are

Tsunami Series of huge waves created when an ocean is affected by an event such as an earthquake or volcanic eruption

Triassic First geological period in the Mesozoic era

Theropod Mainly flesh-eating, two-legged dinosaurs

Vertebrae Bones of the spine

• COLOUR HISTORY •

Colour, Keep & Learn with our exciting Colour Natural History series

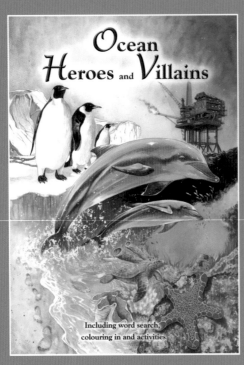

978-0-9542102-6-7

978-1-906475-15-4

Colour History Limited, 30 Moorfields, Raskelf, York YO61 3UZ.
Tel: 01347 824459/8   Fax: 01347 822543
Email: colourhistory@btopenworld.com Web: www.colourhistory.com

ISBN 978-1-906475-15-4

9 781906 475154

The Building Regulations 2000

Conservation of fuel and power

www.tso.co.uk

L2B

**APPROVED
DOCUMENT**

L2B Conservation of fuel and power in existing buildings other than dwellings

Coming into effect 1 October 2010

**2010
edition**

MAIN CHANGES IN THE 2010 EDITION

1. This Approved Document L2B comes into force on 1 October 2010 in support of the Building and Approved Inspectors (Amendment) Regulations 2010, SI 2010 No. 719. The main changes to the legal requirements and the supporting guidance since the issue of the previous Approved Document L2B are as follows:

Changes in the legal requirements

2. The exemption from the energy efficiency provisions for extensions consisting of a conservatory or porch is amended to grant the exemption only where any existing walls, windows or doors are retained, or replaced if removed, and where the heating system of the building is not extended into the conservatory or porch.

3. The list of work in Schedule 2B (work that need not be notified to building control) is amended to include the installation of thermal insulation in a roof space or loft space where this is the only work carried out and the work is not carried out to comply with any requirement in the Building Regulations.

Changes in the technical guidance

4. In this Approved Document the guidance is generally based upon an elemental approach to demonstrating compliance, with additional guidance that provides greater flexibility. The main technical changes comprise a general strengthening of energy efficiency standards that are considered reasonable for work on thermal elements, controlled fittings and controlled services in existing buildings.

5. Amended guidance is given for historic and traditional buildings which may have an exemption from the energy efficiency requirements or where special considerations apply.

6. Amended guidance is given where an extension is a conservatory or porch that is not exempt from the energy efficiency requirements.

7. The guidance for the renovation of a thermal element through the provision of a new layer or through the replacement of an existing layer has been expanded.

8. Guidance is provided for swimming pool basins (walls and floor) in existing buildings.